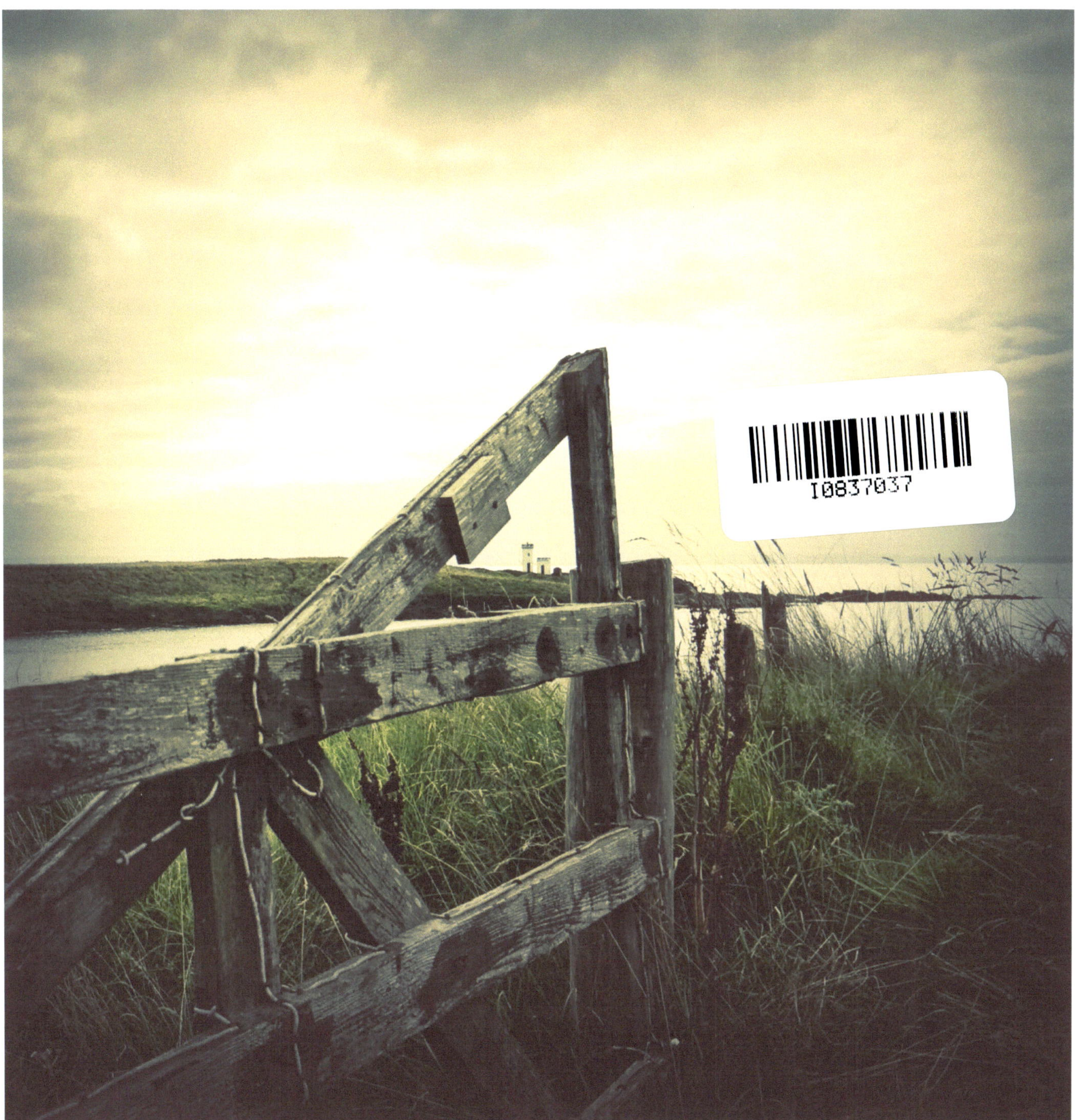

Paul A Dickens - Author

Paul Dickens was born in Edinburgh and he still lives and works between there and the East Neuk of Fife, drawing huge amounts of inspiration from both town and country environments, 'two of the most inspiring places to be'. These two differing but equally beautiful parts of Scotland allow him to indulge some of his passions in life.

"I adore nature, wildlife and bird watching and try to marry the natural world and its scenery into my feelings and compare the beauty and simplicity of nature, landscapes and the sea in and around Fife to the complexity of living in Edinburgh in the modern world."

Paul is married to Kathleen and has a daughter, Charlie. He adores being a husband and a father and cites watching his daughter Charlie growing up, and her childlike observations of life, as one of his other major inspirations.

He has been writing poetry since he was ten years old and this is his first book.

Juile Tinton - Photographer

After many years working in Hong Kong's financial sector, Julie returned to Scotland to exploit her creative talents. "Photography has always been a big part of my life but initially, I regarded it as nothing more than a passionate hobby and great way to express myself.

When making a decision as to what do with the rest of my life – friends and family persuaded me to jump a million miles out of my comfort zone and go back to the classroom to set me on my way to become a 'bona fide' professional photographer. That was 7 years ago and I've never looked back!

Photography is so much more than my profession. I truly love what I do!"

Julie lives in Edinburgh with her two young sons, Josh and Robbie.

View Julie's portfolio at www.julietinton.com

For Mayame, Kathleen, Charlie and all my sisters

for being there when I need you,
which is basically all the time

PD xxx

Contents

Through a Shutter 9
Flesh from a Rainbow 11
The Geese Arrive 13
A Village or a City 15
The Petal 17
Sunnyside 19
A Sea in December 21
The Kestrel from Crail 23
The Blackbird's Song 25
For My Child 27
The Cormorant 29
Saint Laurent De Corbierre 31
The Winter Crocus 33
A Stone Façade in Brugge 35
Walking to the Wall 37
Looking for Shelter 39
The First Swallow in April 41
To Lose a View 43
Who She Is! 45
In the Wrong Place 47
The Confidence of Autumn 49
Without Darkness 51
The Season Who Lied 53
The Mood of Winter 55
To Divorce a City 57

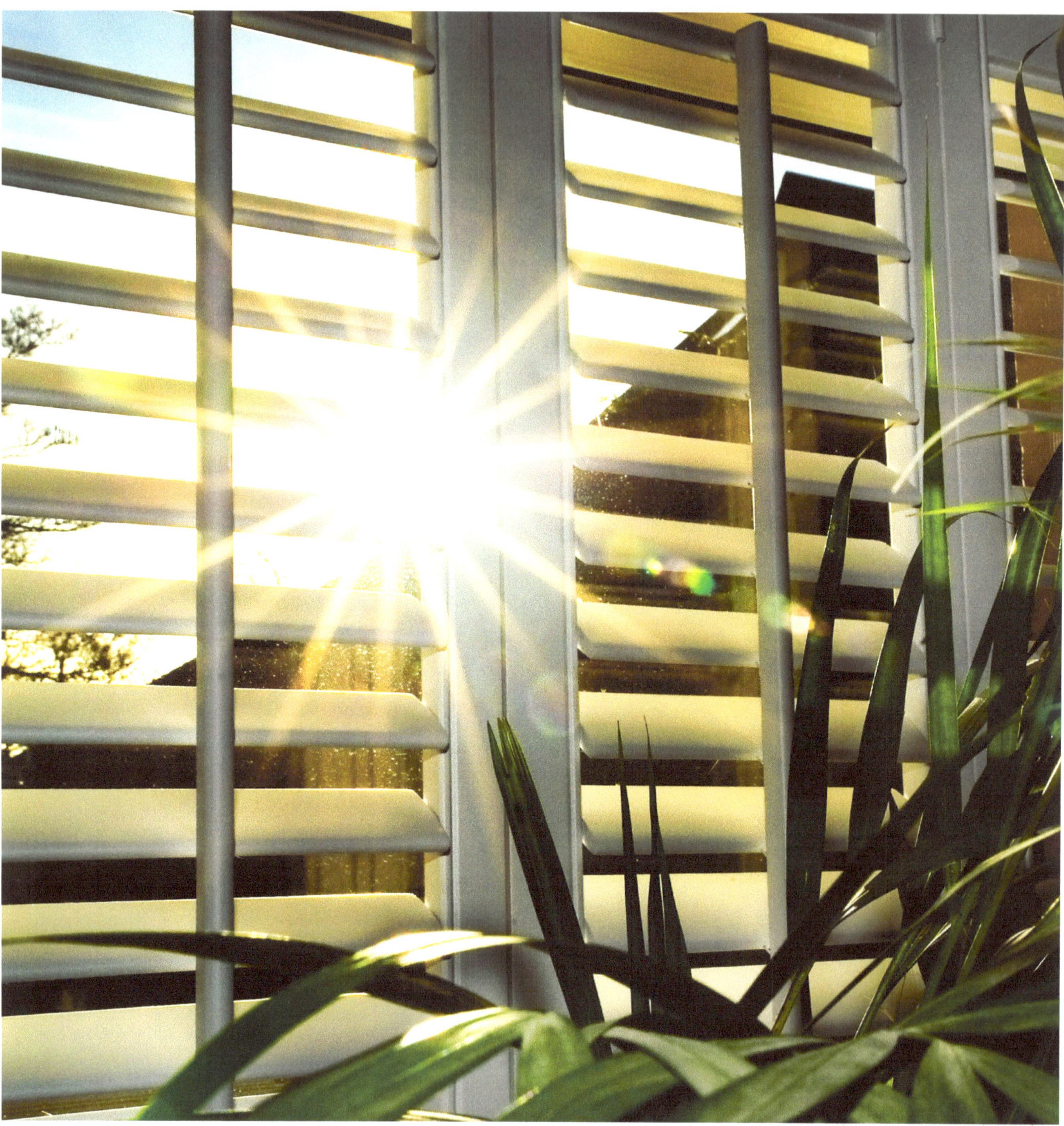

Through a Shutter

The morning light might as well have been a season away!

Minutes traded, thought after thought, and soon an hour was born, leaving every lock vulnerable, without a key, and anyone could now visit the inside, depositing opinions and shallow dreams upon a solitude who had become confused without any light.

Daylight began to creep through the shutter, as waves teased a troubled mind, inch by inch.

Her hand found mine, even though she was still asleep, caressed my hand, chasing away demon after demon.

For Kathleen

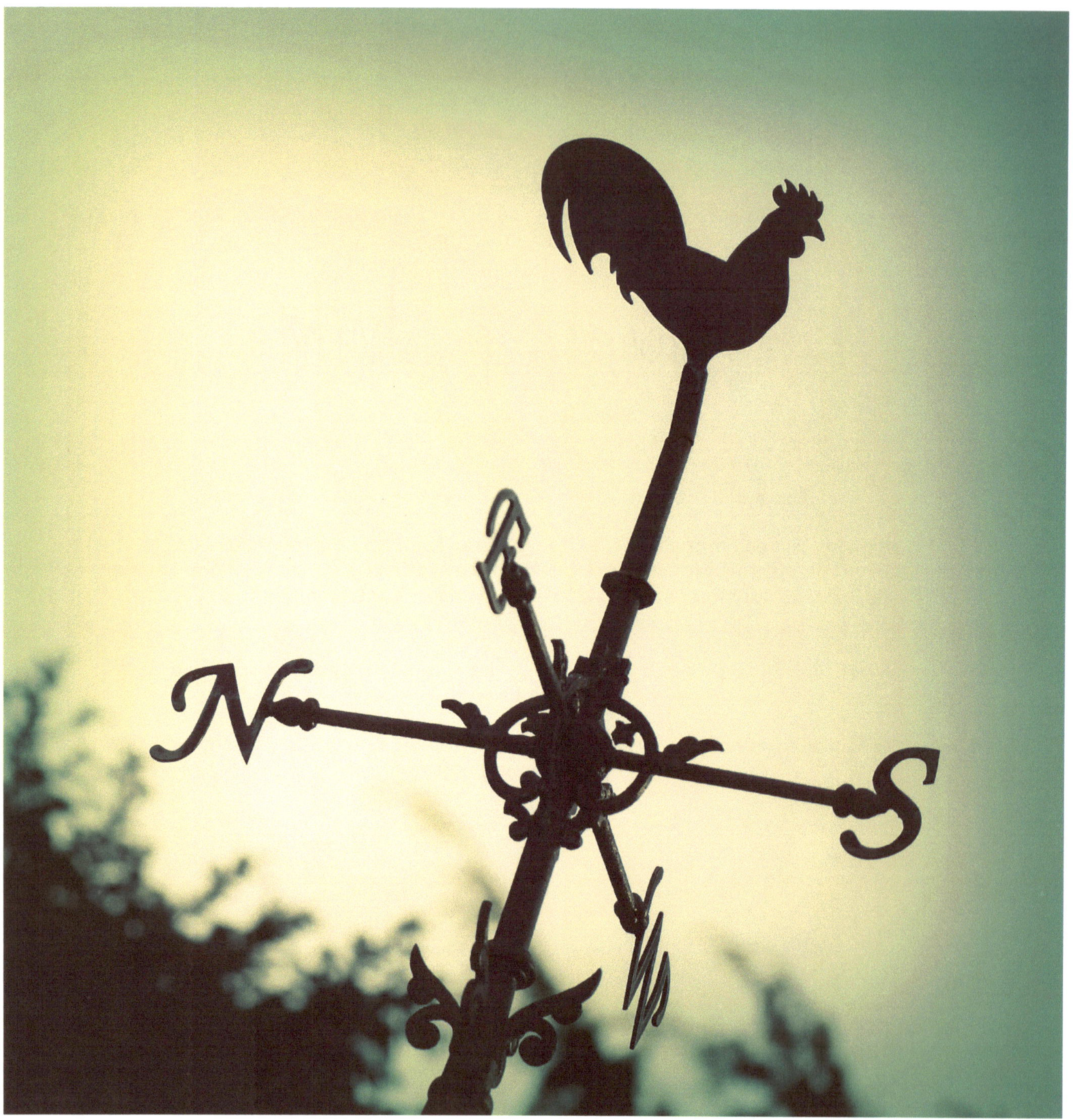
N
S

Flesh from a Rainbow

The winds cut the flesh from a rainbow, stealing her colours for a black-and-white heart.

The new colours tried to introduce themselves, but could not be heard, seen or felt.

A weathercock spun in the distance, pointing to whatever it wants and, upon finding a straw, christened it justice!

The clouds and skies, who are parents to us all, and keepers of time, looked down to the seas, who itself was an orphan to everything that ever breathed or pleaded mortality.

The waters continued to smack the shore with a renewed confidence!

The flesh from the rainbow that did not belong in its new home, pleaded to become a colour for all to be seen, and never again to be concealed by the shadows of a colourless heart.

The weathercock ceased to spin, questioning the colours of its own heart!

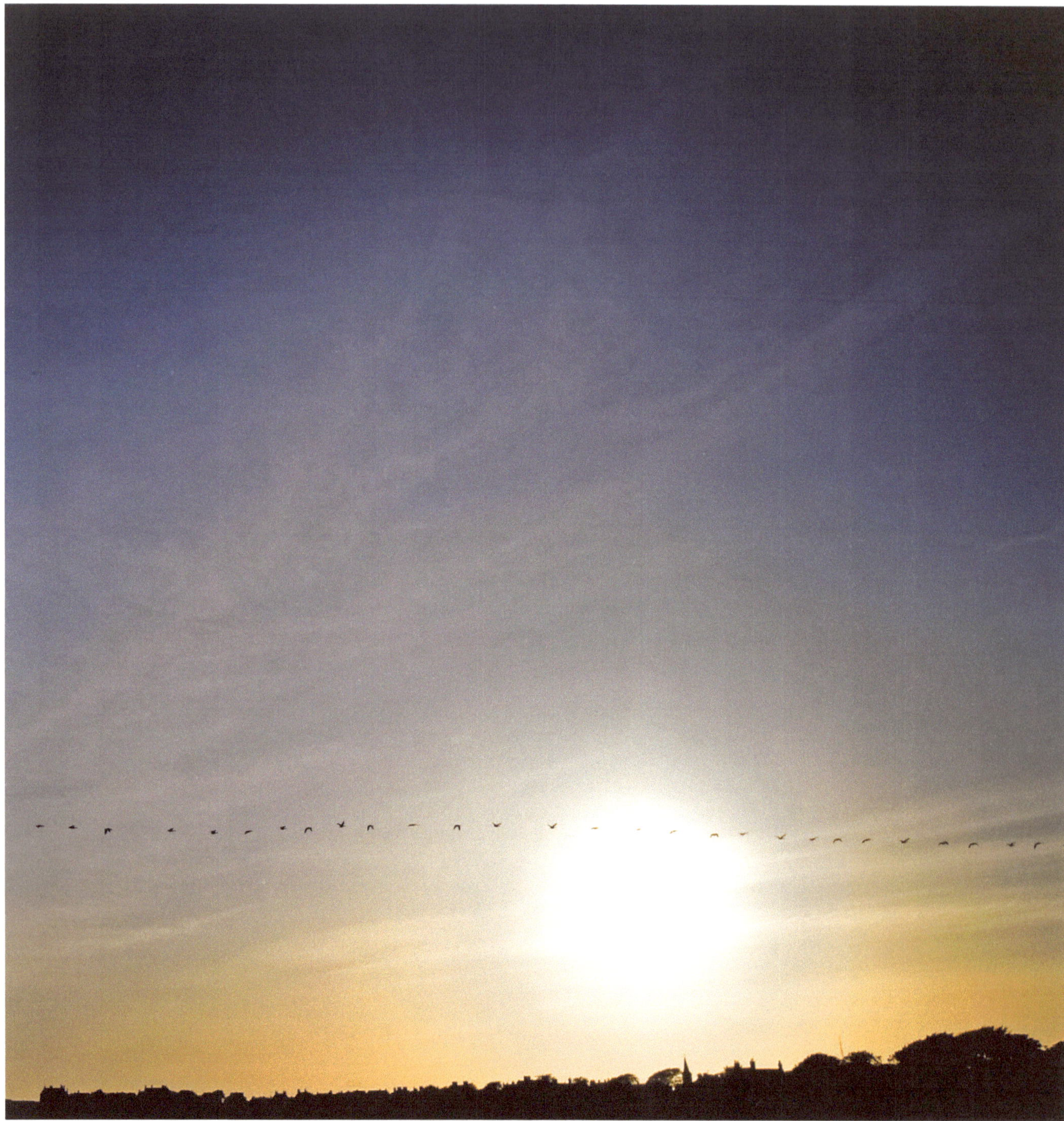

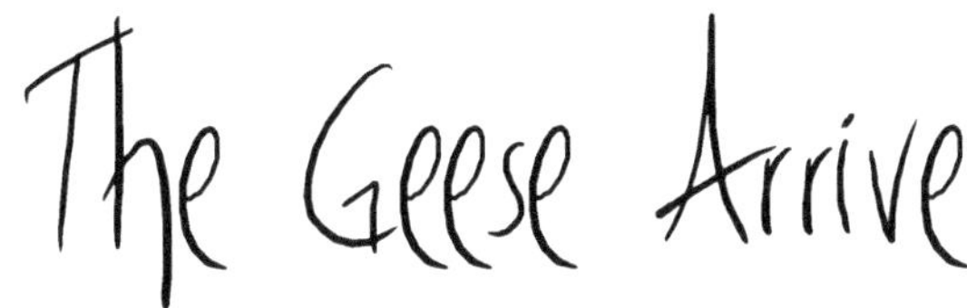

The Geese Arrive

Before they landed, or selected their home, they scribbled some charcoal in the sky, and dusk began her shift.

Thousands of them had descended on a field who, having anticipated their visit, had sold all her wheat, leaving the once-gold stalks trimmed to a beard.

They fussed, flapped and argued before settling in their home, which was an instant village outside a village.

Within minutes their confidence was complete and they were no longer outsiders and, with the gathering nearly complete, they stamped their feet and looked at each other. It was not clear at this stage which one would deliver the sermon.

In a neighbouring field, a plough had delivered miles of anxiety, creating furrows filled with frowns.

A tribe of curlews, shaking with optimism, chiselled at the frowns, testing their sense of humour by the minute, and investigating every crumb the soil had to offer.

Over the hedge, nine herons held a conference, with shoulders shrugged; they debated the arrival of the new immigrants.

With a complete silence, the debate was over.

Witnessing three fields, so apart and so together, I left them all to their various debates.

They had not seen me; I would never forget them!

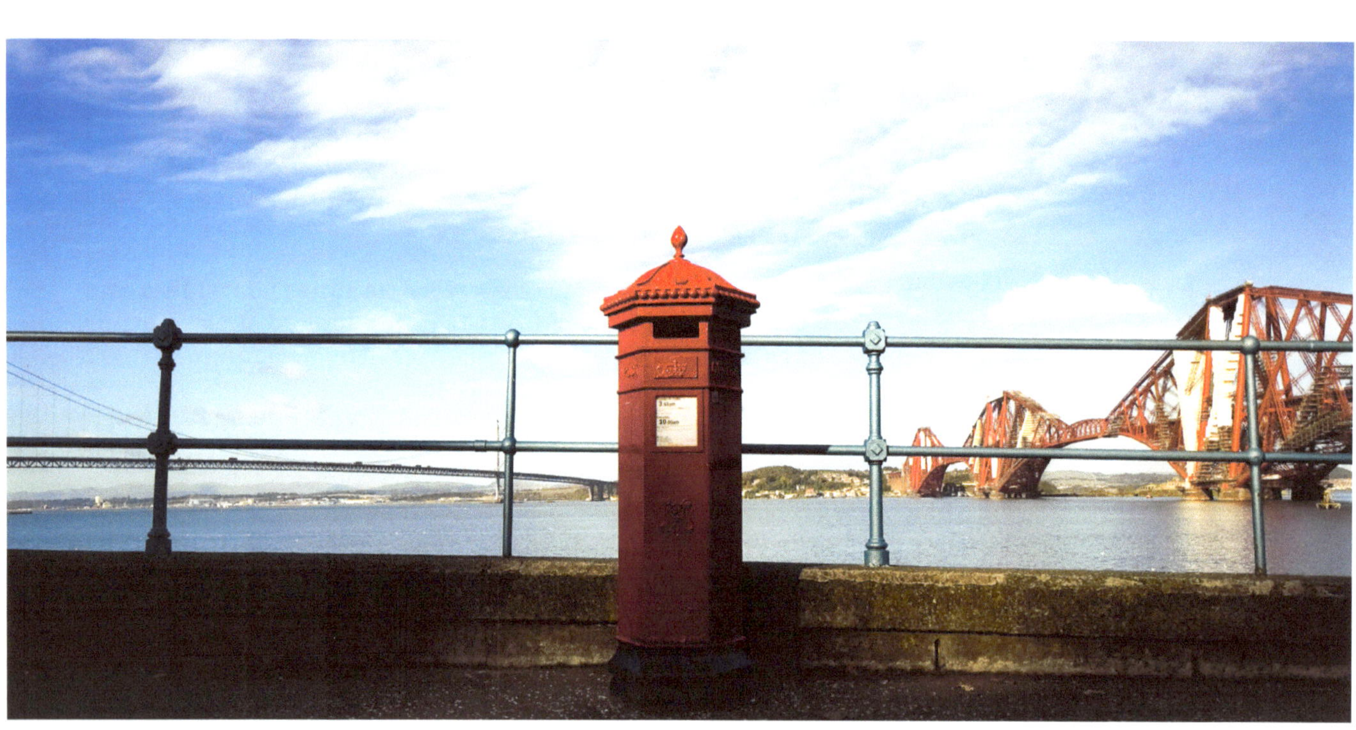

A Village or a City

Do I belong to a village or a city?

I need to belong to someone, forever, a landscape or a building I can call mine; it has to be filled with laughter and friendship, who will never question the false price of gold I used to own.

Is it a village or a city that will listen to me, or do I have to whisper forever, and question every window with a blind or a twitching curtain stating, "You are not what we want you to be"?

Do I belong to a village or a city?

Which one will be the first to open the curtains and blinds and let true light shine through?

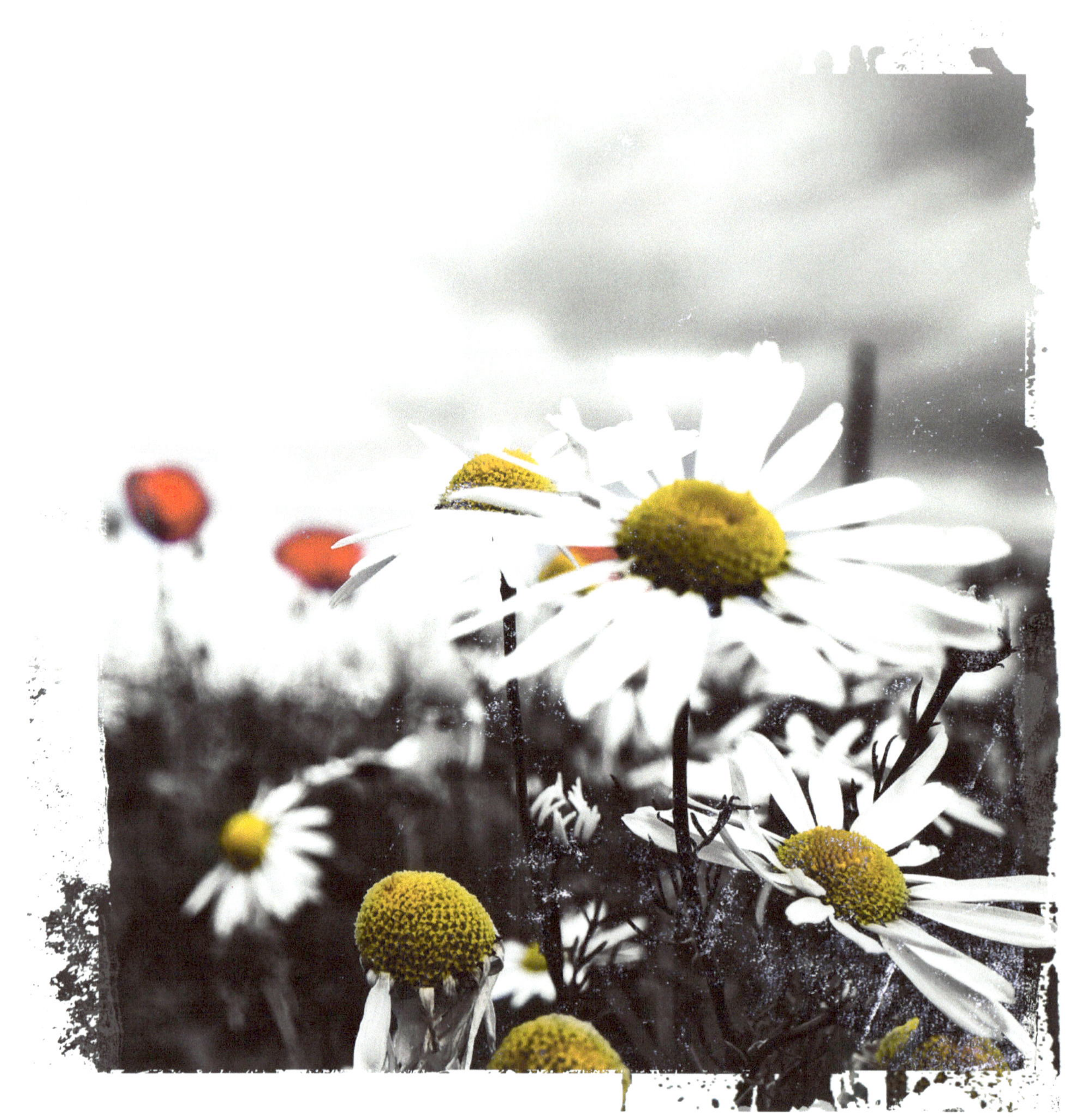

The Petal

A flower, full of pride, paraded her petals, like signets around her neck!

Insecure of how long they will need her, she whispered that they were the finest colours she had ever made! Or had ever owned!

Borrowing some salt from God, she made a tear from the sea, and shed the liquid over the petals, in the hope they may last a minute longer!

The courage of the petals' temporary death hung in a cloud and, as her colours bled, the season had become bored with this debate, and moved on!

The petal shivered, not knowing if it would own a colour next season!

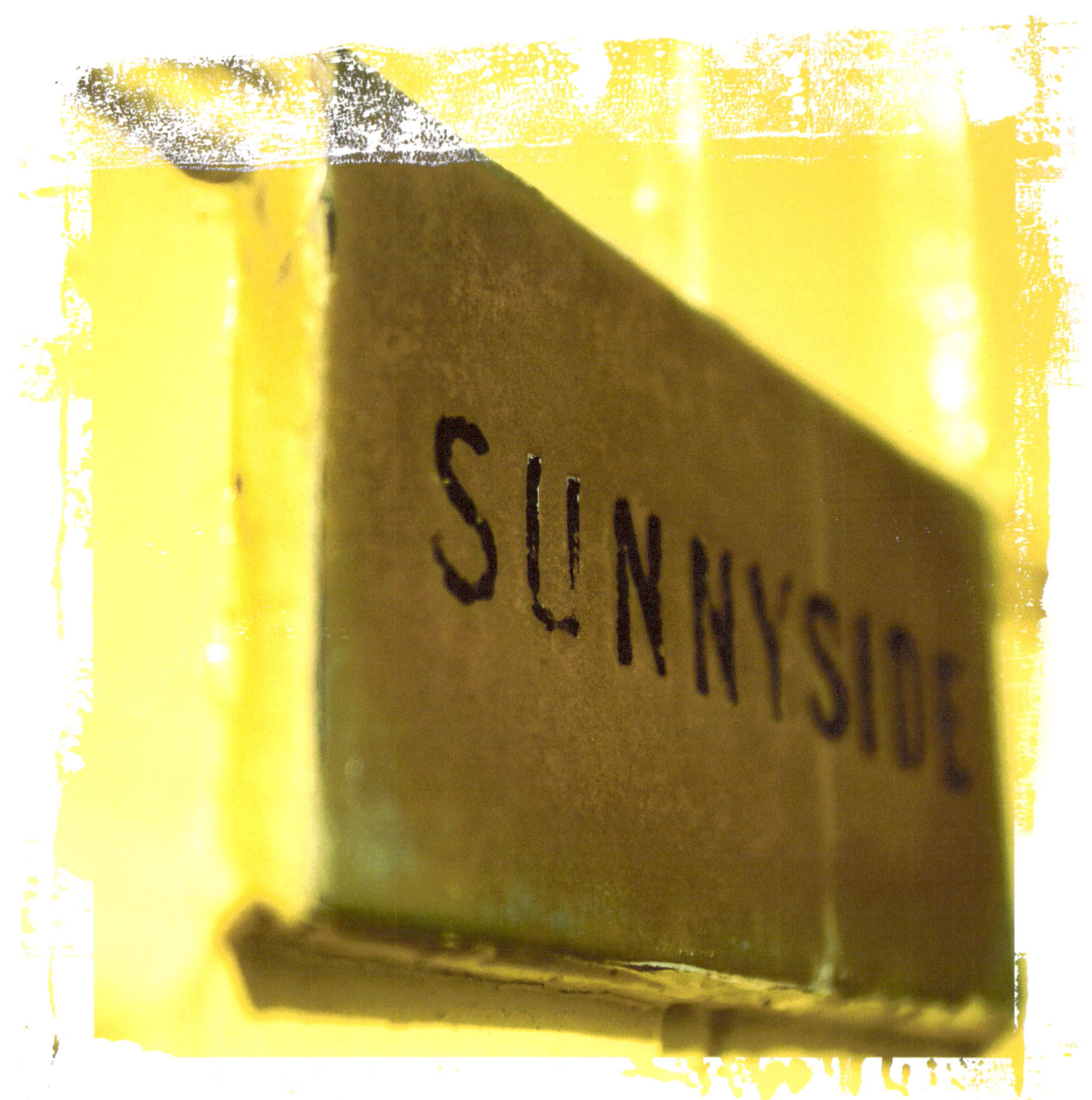
SUNNYSIDE

Sunnyside

As the tide deserted me, another came in, taking control of every grain of sand I had ever owned.

Reflecting on my loss, I borrowed a segment of time, to steal or to borrow a view.

I was deemed to be only a passerby and posed no threat to mortality, views, tides or anything, and was therefore granted to be able to borrow a segment of nothing!

This nothing I now possessed became everything I had ever seen, or wanted!

The stolen view became restless in my eyes, and returned to dance with the tides, where it belonged and where it would stay.

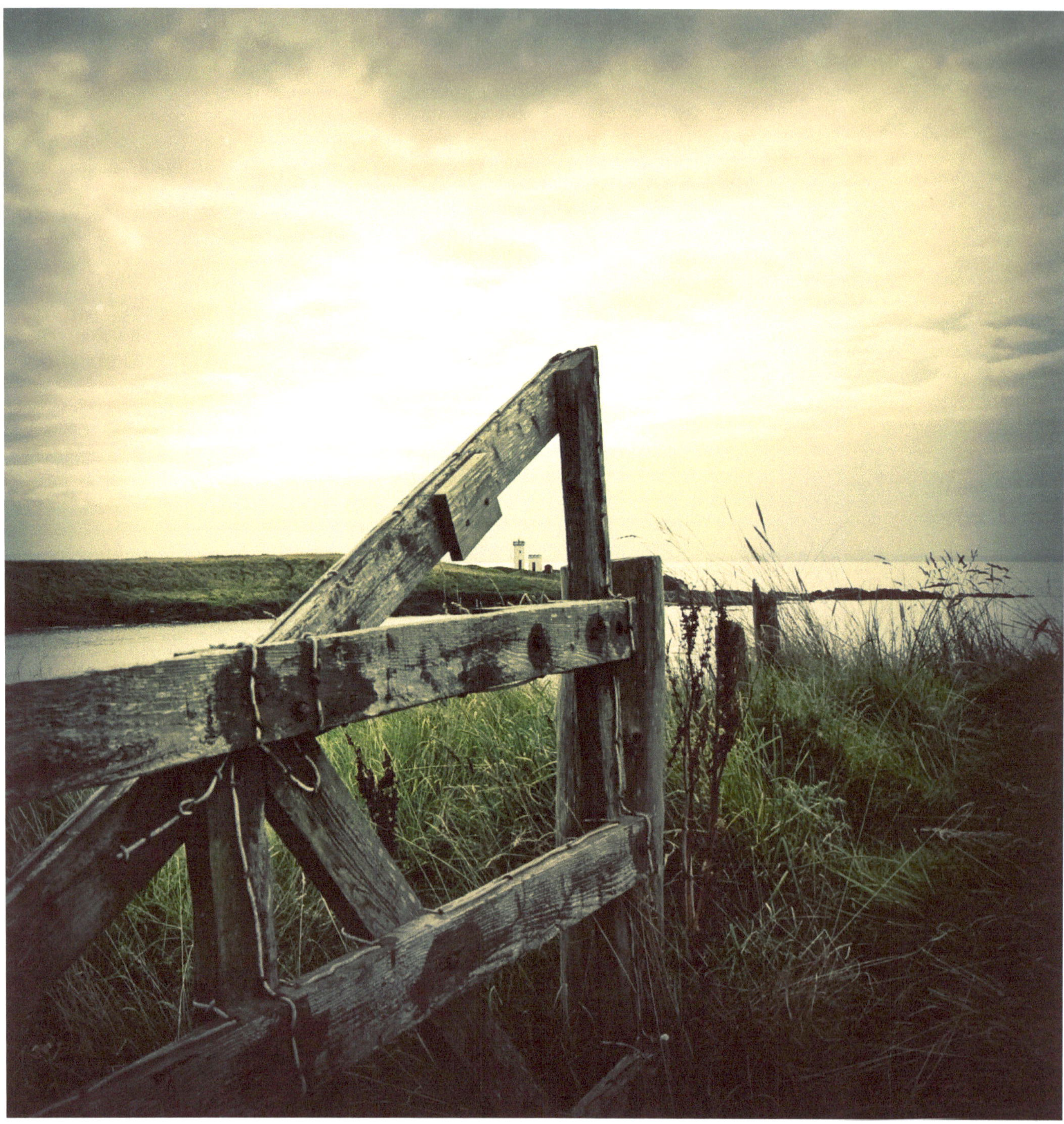

A Sea in December

The sea was simply furious with everyone, and everything that surrounded her!

No-one could get a word in edgeways!

The rocks on the coast had begun to question their own confidence and began to concentrate on survival in itself, trying to hold their own ground as the white froth, dressed in a rage, challenged their mortality.

A harvest of power continued to roar and hypnotise all that was around; the noise was alive with anything it wanted to hear.

Beyond the front line of the crashing waves, somewhere against the very skin of the land, a trawler struggled in the distance, looking to catch hope, or a calm!

It would be many hours before this sea would sleep.

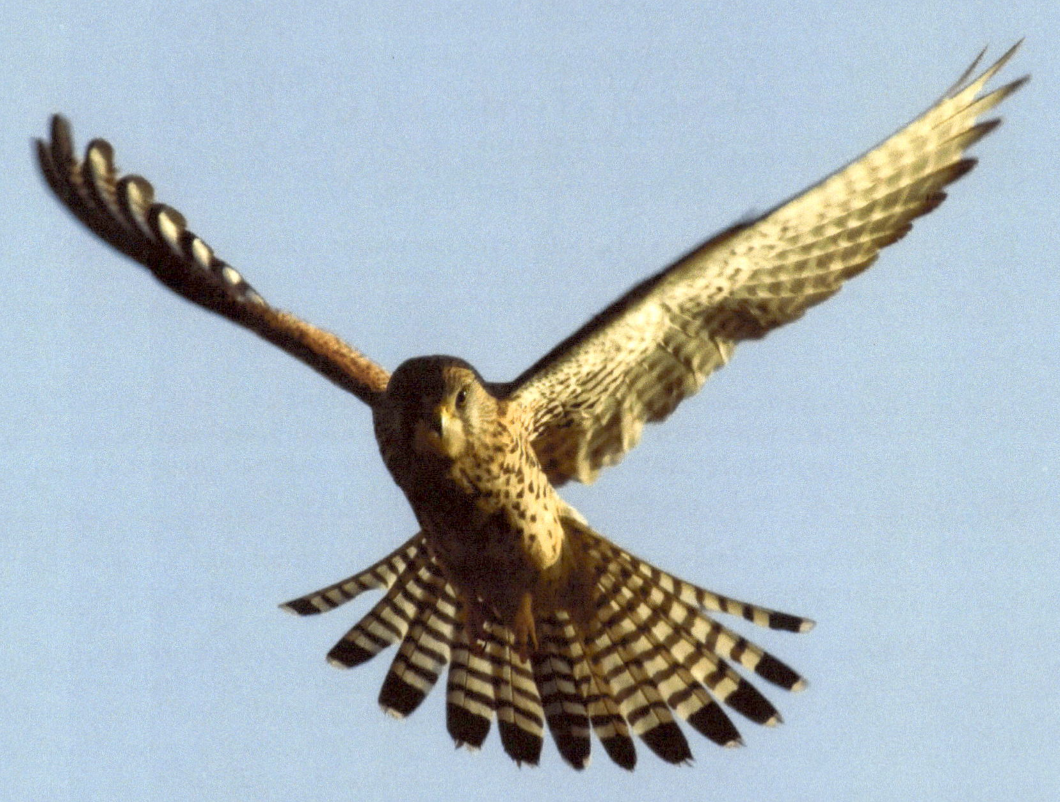

The Kestrel from Crail

Away from where I should be, I stared at 60 sparrows in a Majorcan tree, gossiping and arguing about the time of day.

Their confidence was high, and their colours were simple and clear.

They were what they were, and carried on noticing nothing except themselves!

Back home, a single kestrel hovered against an East Neuk wind and, with not a friend to be seen, he relentlessly controlled his own loneliness.

Back in the tree, the sparrows had overcrowded their space, and their conference had broken into an argument!

The kestrel would remain alone, and was grateful for the colours he had. He had accepted loneliness was not an option, but a way of life!

The sparrows left their tree, one by one.

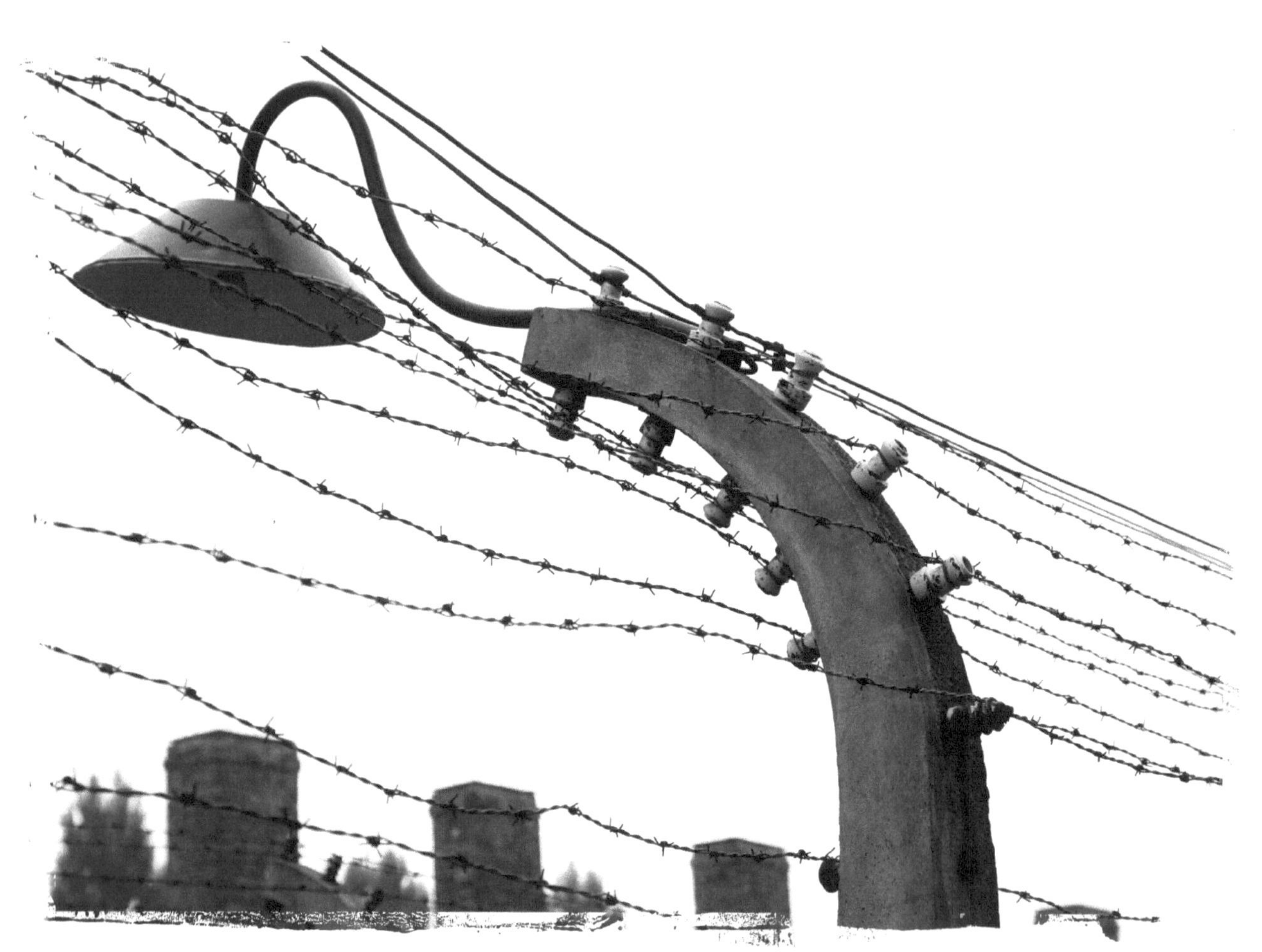

The Blackbird's Song

Death, refusing to die, lingered all around.

The blackbird closed his eyes and sang.

Refusing to be forgotten, and with train tracks laid by Judas, he sang to every conscience known to us all.

A bouquet of guilt, wrapped in a barbed-wire rose, refused to hide a truth from the blackbird's song, where the silence sang loudest!

Cruelty has no limits, it would appear.

Shame on the bricks and the roofs that have no heart, which sheltered evil for so long, their own consciences poisoned by a gas long ago.

Not a colour could be recognised.

The blackbird's song became louder
from a watchtower, singing the truth, hard to imagine,
impossible to ignore.

The song was loud and pure, reflecting everything I should never have seen.

Written in Auschwitz and Berkendau Concentration Camps, Poland
- no words will ever be enough!

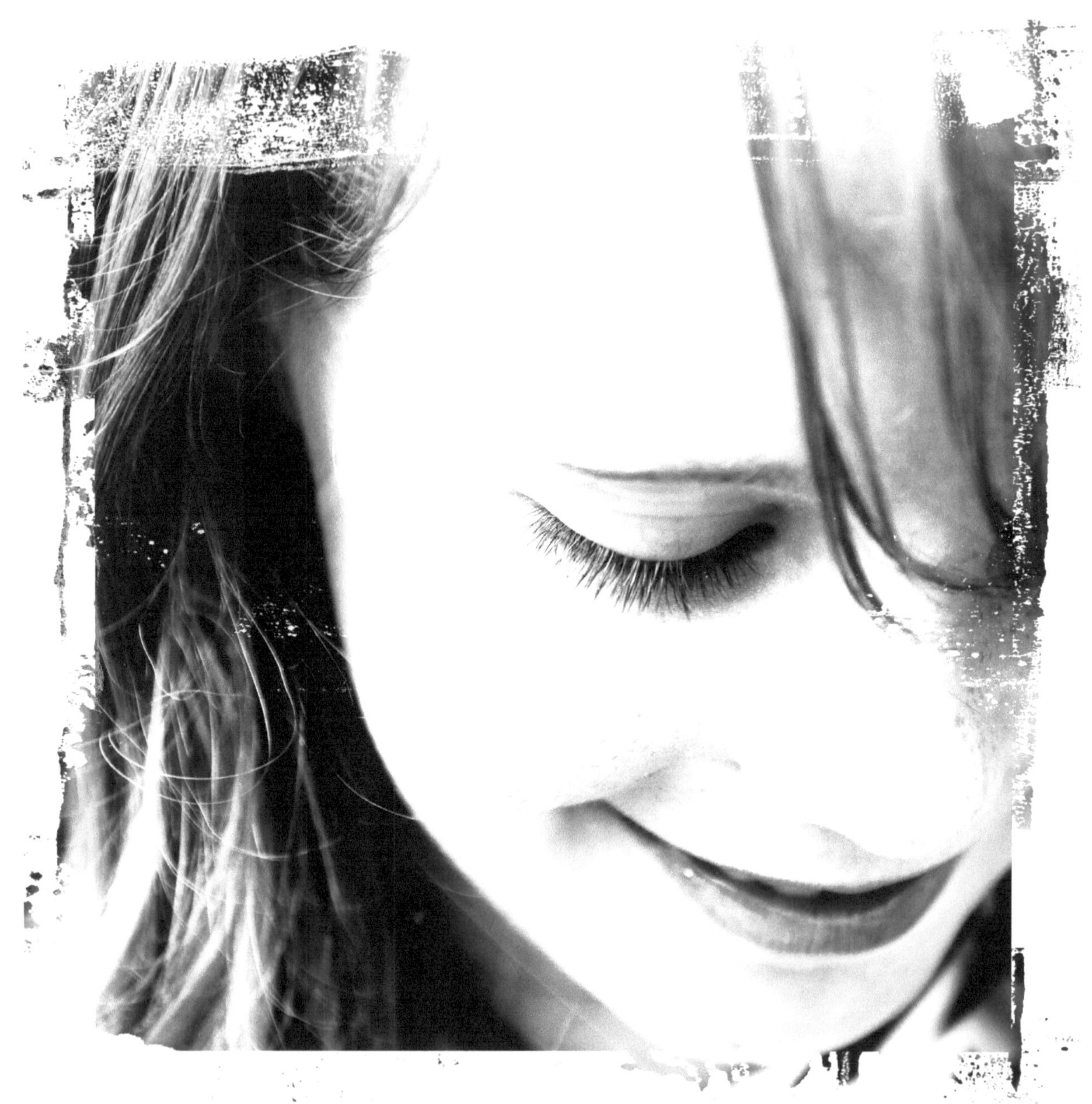

For My Child

Sow your sorrows between the lines in my face; I will grow them and keep you free from pain.

I will harvest them when you are asleep, and scatter their petals forever.

Give me all your tears of yesterday and forever; I will drink them so you will never drown.

Give me your doubts or clouds that prevent you from being you, and from being what you are; I will throw them to the coast, which will break them up.

This will leave you as you are, the most beautiful landscape in my life!

For Charlie, love Dad, '09

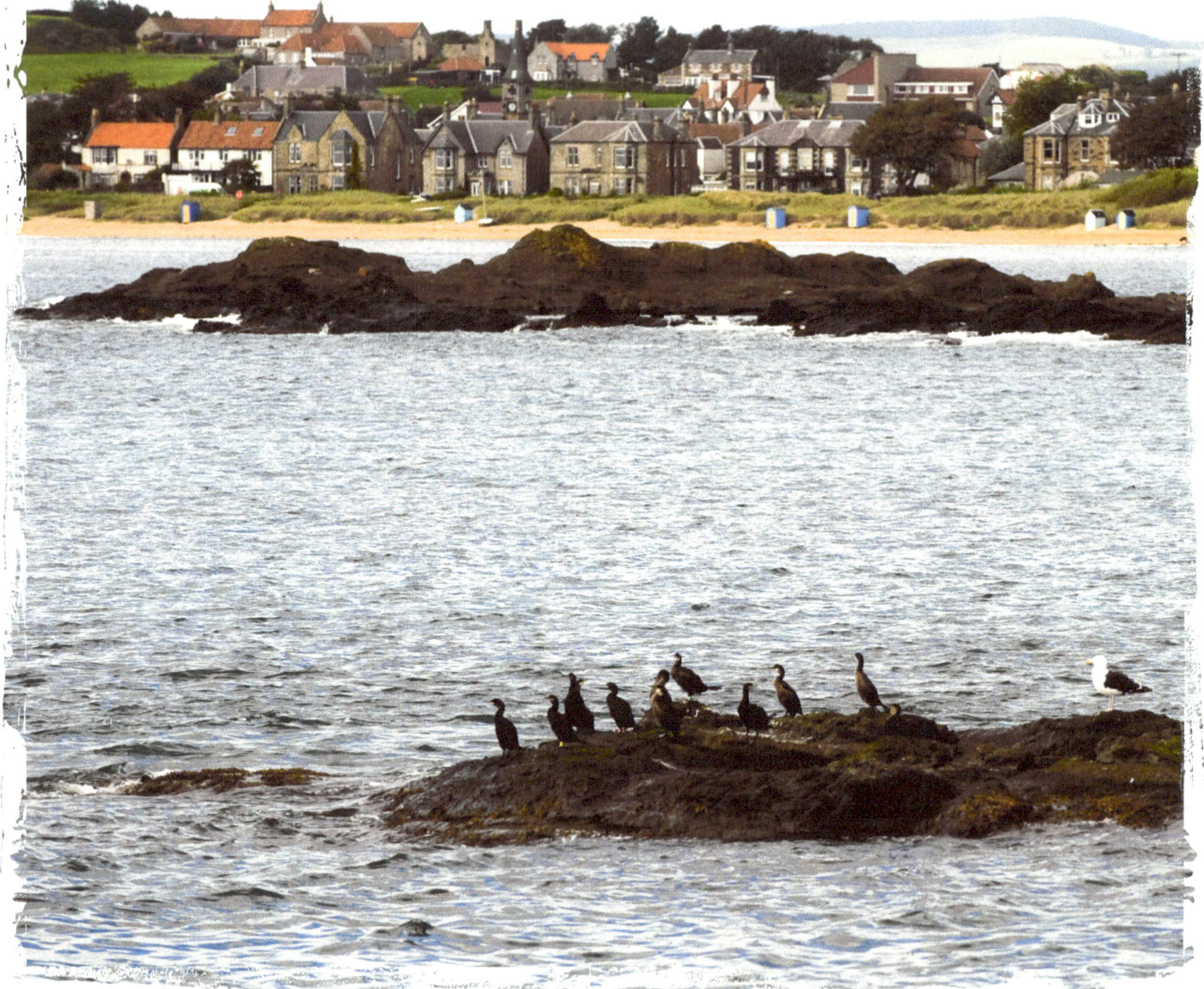

The Cormorant

The cormorant lay flat and crumpled on the sand.

Her life finished, laid to rest by some pebbles which, as if in a trance, followed the tide everywhere it went!

The sea crackled and laughed at all that was mortal.

The blue, cloudless sky shared that same belief, albeit in a more serene and less boastful manner.

Behind the tomb of sand, six herons stood like silver statues and, through eyes like yellow splinters, they gathered all they needed to see, focused and cold.

The sea continued to crackle and gazed at everything it wanted.

What could I see? Amongst all this nature, I was a hopeless tourist.

I turned to my two spaniel companions who saw nothing and were only capable of sniffing every pebble in sight!

The lighthouse caught my eye! A potential friend?

His eye was too focused and of no need of a companion.

Not today, not ever!

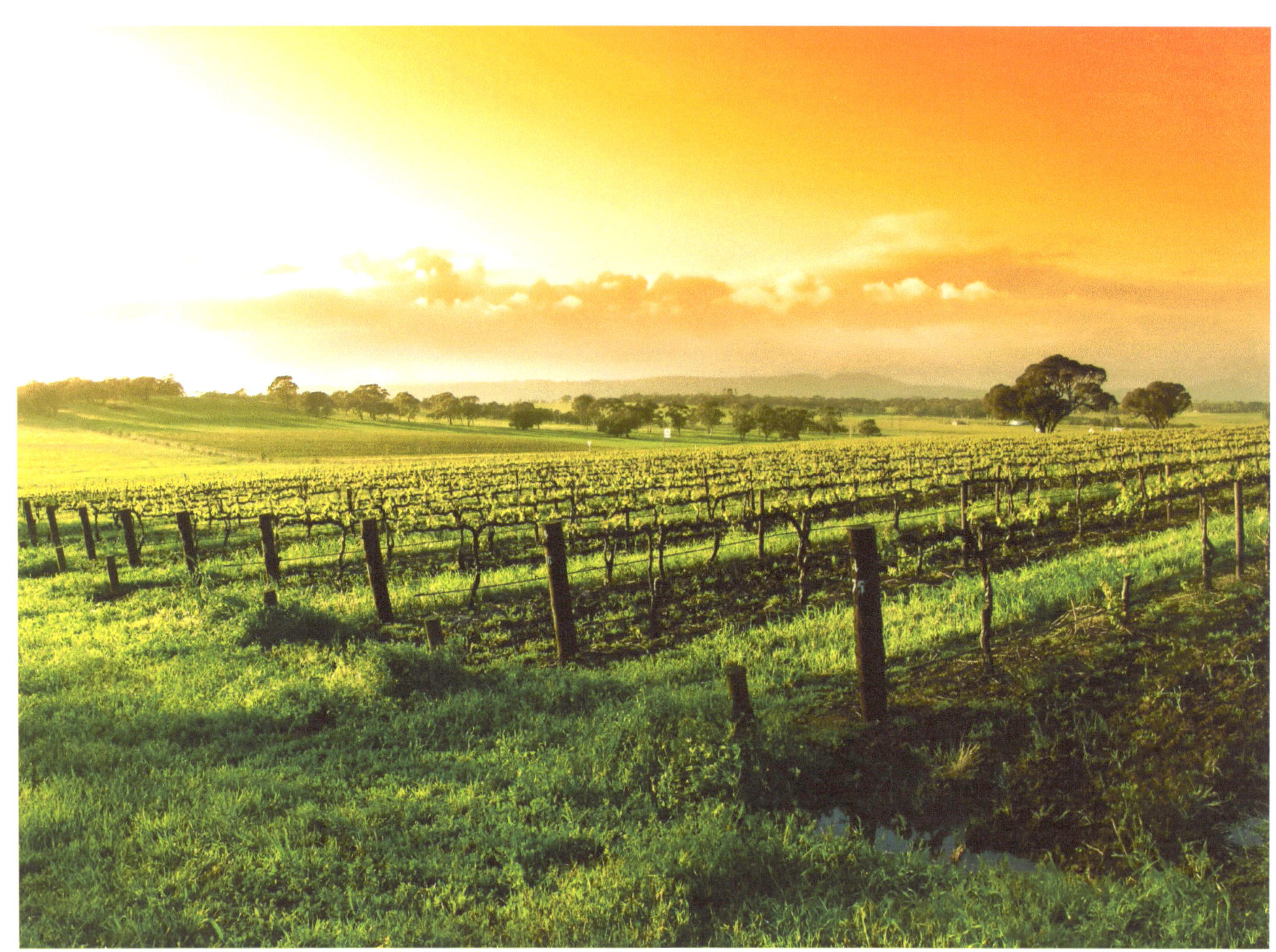

Saint Laurent de Corbiere

A face carved from a leather landscape poured me a glass of red.

Lavender clouds spilled smiles from village to village.

Rows of vineyards took their positions in avenues of confidence,
knowing tomorrow they would be even more strong and beautiful.

A church bell rang to remind me God would be awake soon.

Would he speak to me today?

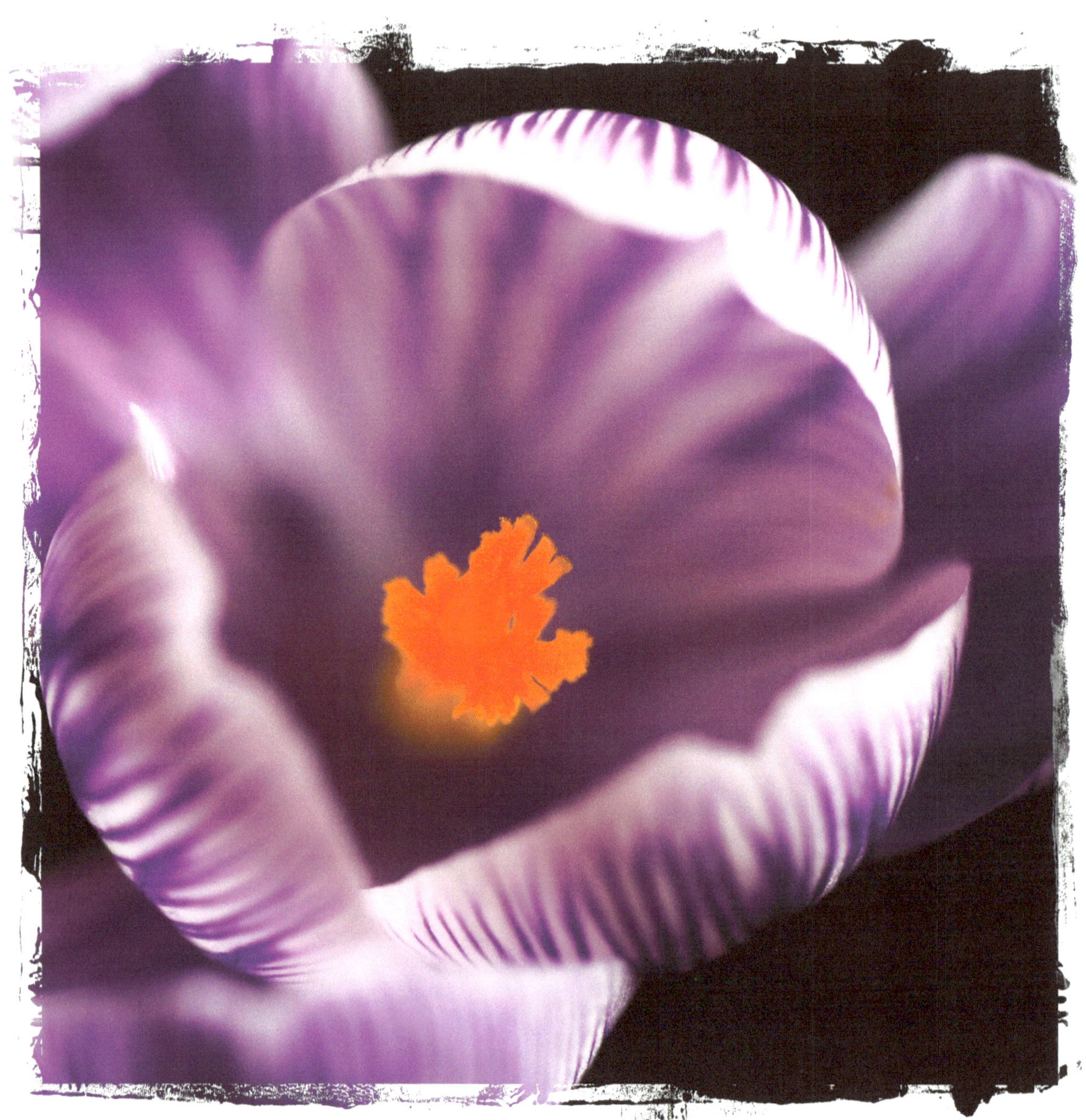

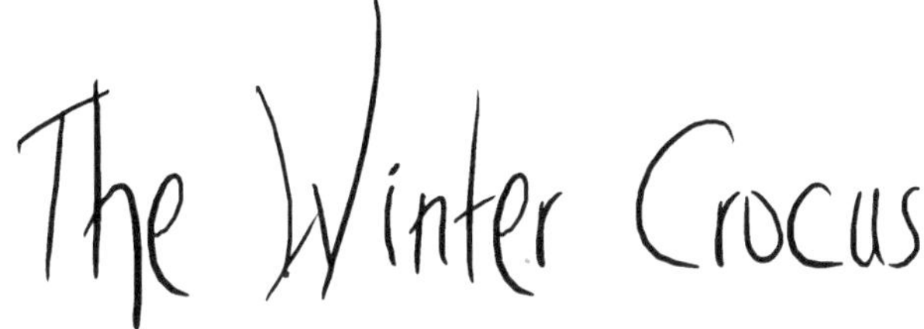

The Winter Crocus

The winter crocus borrowed my garden, offering petals like skin to anyone that wanted to see her.

The trees had lost their families and friends and they now rested on a lawn, kissing another season farewell.

The orchard too braced himself for a lonely winter and, without as much as a blackbird to talk to, he realised he had friends only when fruit was being conceived.

The colour of the winter crocus had become brighter and more confident; she was the queen of my garden.

Maybe the garden was mine, but it was I who had become a trespasser in her short and beautiful life.

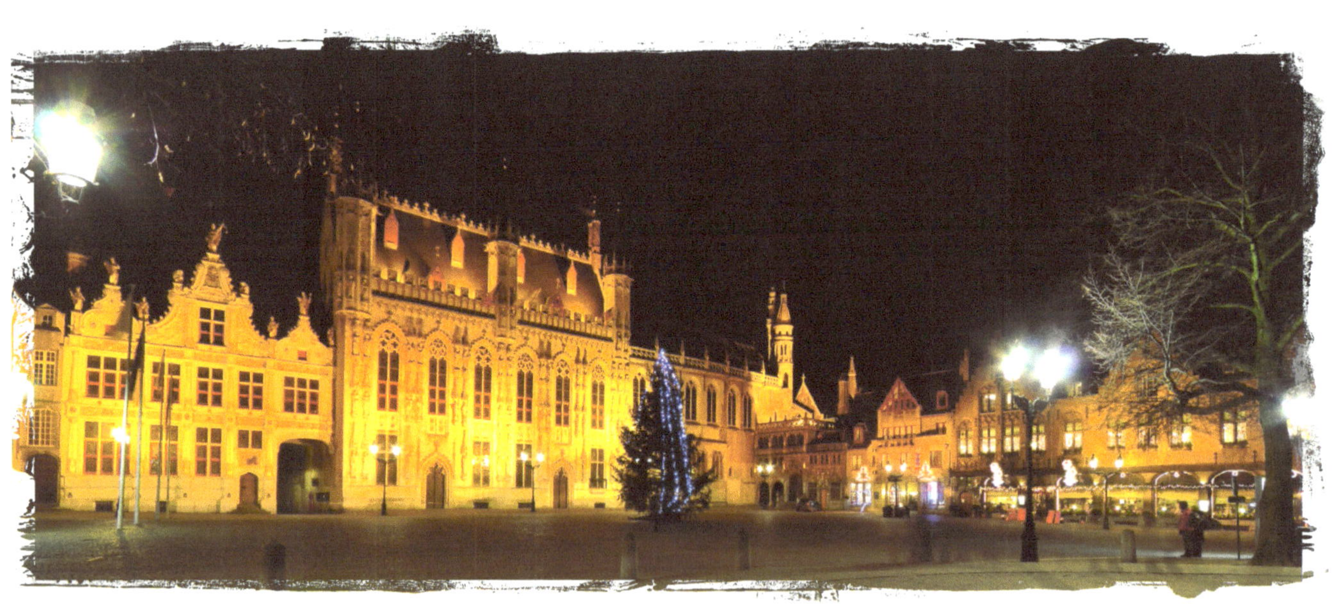

A Stone Façade in Brugge

The towers, steeples and bells were high above, knowing me for what I am, beneath them, without a voice.

The canals were arteries in a dormant mood, no intention of becoming a river. Calmness was not in a hurry; why should it?

Stone façades were all around; no ghosts today!

They were what they were, not lonely, only alone casting their eyes on those who couldn't see.

I caught a glimpse or a reflection of what they were, or perhaps of what I could be!

They will be there next year, the stone façades of Brugge, with their beauty and all that they can see

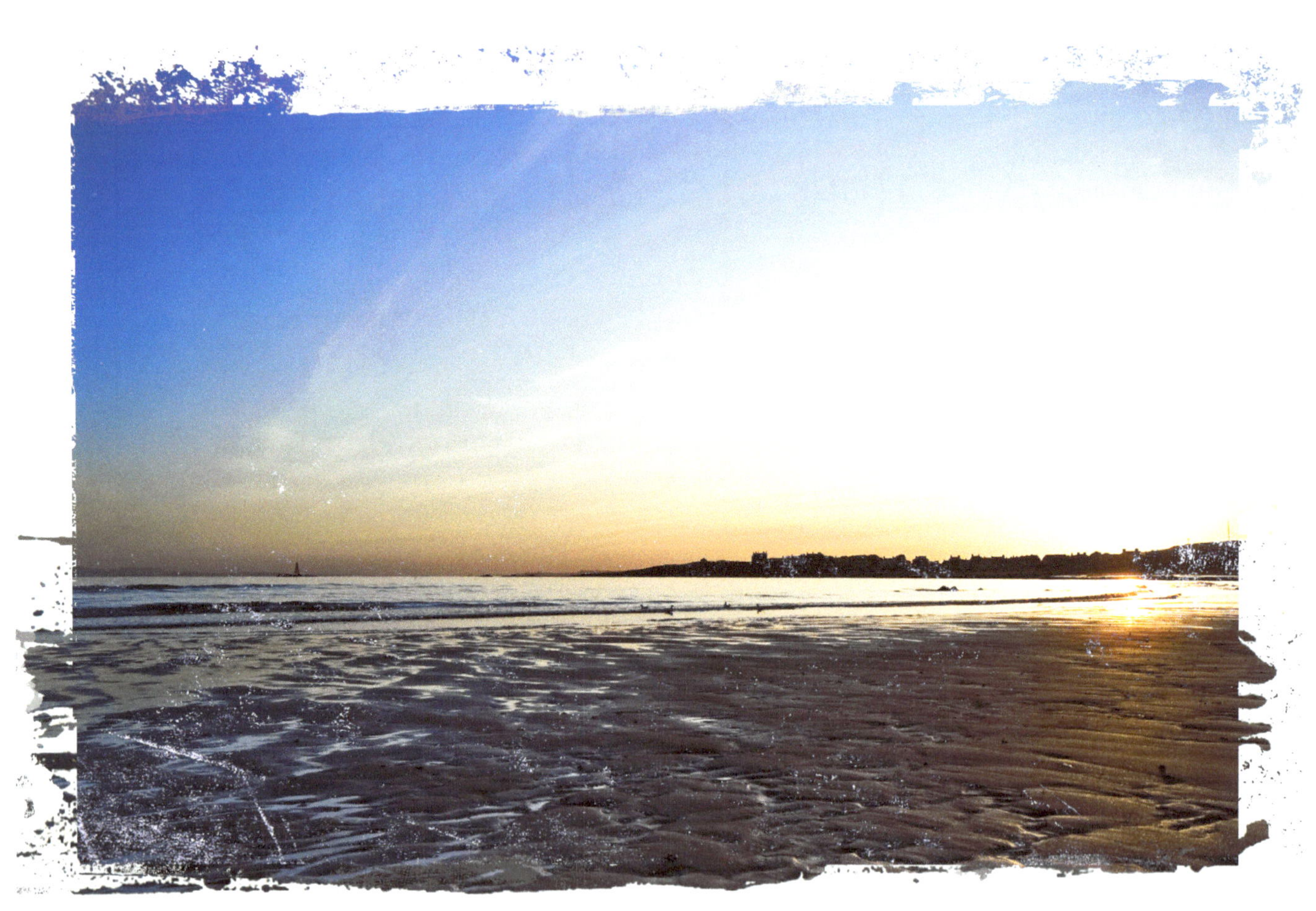

Walking to the Wall

With no-one to talk to, alone, but not lonely, their differences were becoming closer!

Becoming aware of their relationship I split them up, step by step and grain by grain, to allow the lazy eye of the lighthouse to cast judgement!

A piece of driftwood appeared, whose timetable was youthful and immortal, but blinked to witness a young tree robbed from its roots and dying on the shore!

They shared the same blood, but the driftwood returned to her timetable.

The washed-up tree remained in the sands.

The tide had made her decision.

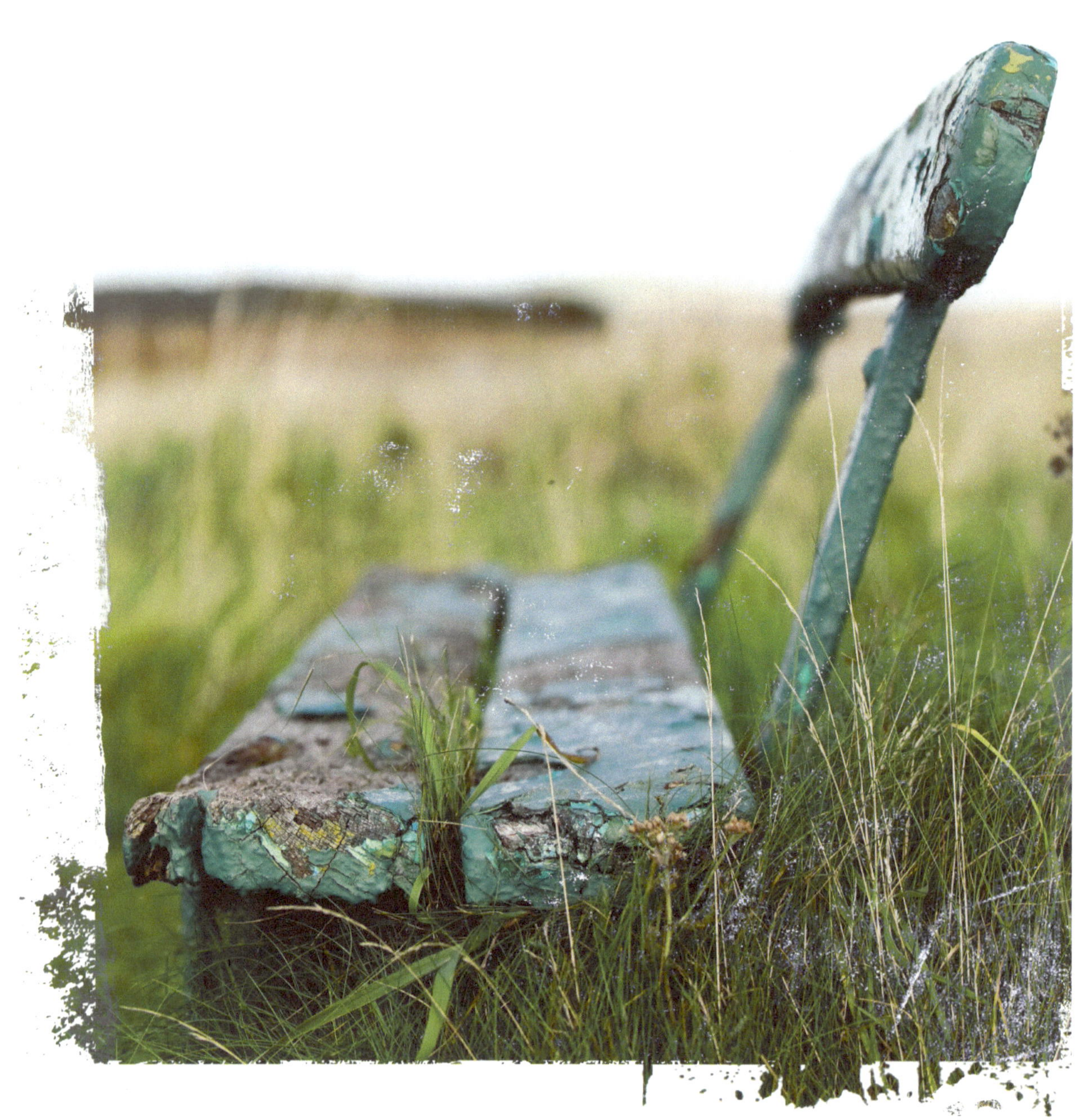

Looking for Shelter

When I cannot hold you, I can see nothing, not myself, not
even the darkness of the night.

I clutch to your warmth, and pray for a calm that will carry
me to you again.

But tonight you are far away, making time stilted and
without urgency.

Powerless hands tick, without a dance or a purpose.

What gives you the power to control my thoughts?

Your memories, like rain, fall upon me; and I drink them
with a hunger.

When will you be back in my arms to make up for all the lost
moments and feed me back to reality?

Please shelter my love, and breathe everything I can give.

I have come home; I am yours, totally yours; believe in me
and give me shelter and let the clock of love continue.

For Kathleen

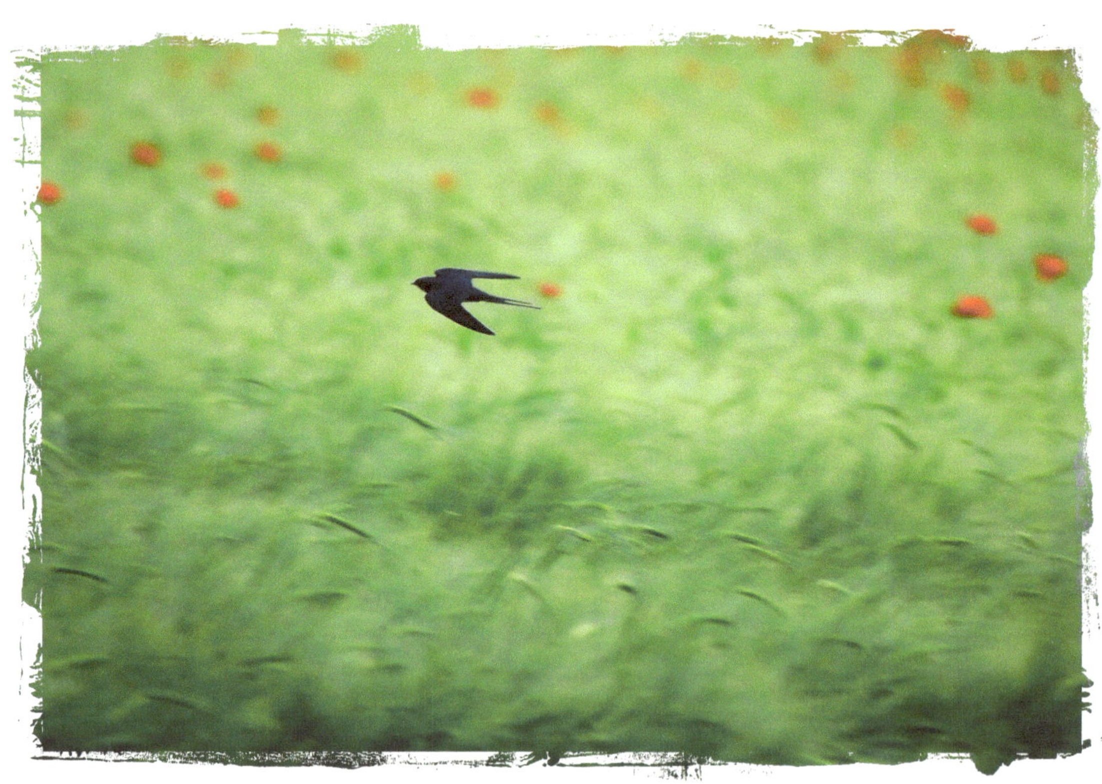

The First Swallow in April

The swallow arrived like a dart, ice skating in the spring air, spelling out that energy had arrived!

This ballet did not want to sleep.

Dusk too had fallen for her charms and colours, and delayed the nightfall for another 20 minutes, so another encore could be witnessed.

In the morning the swallow had plans to stitch a hammock to the side of my house and, when this would be completed, the perfect sculpture would portray the house as a mere small extension to her sleeping and breeding place.

The receding tide had no audience and, for the first time, jealously engulfed her shores.

She longed for the end of September when the swallow's ballet would be over, and her own beauty would perhaps be needed once more.

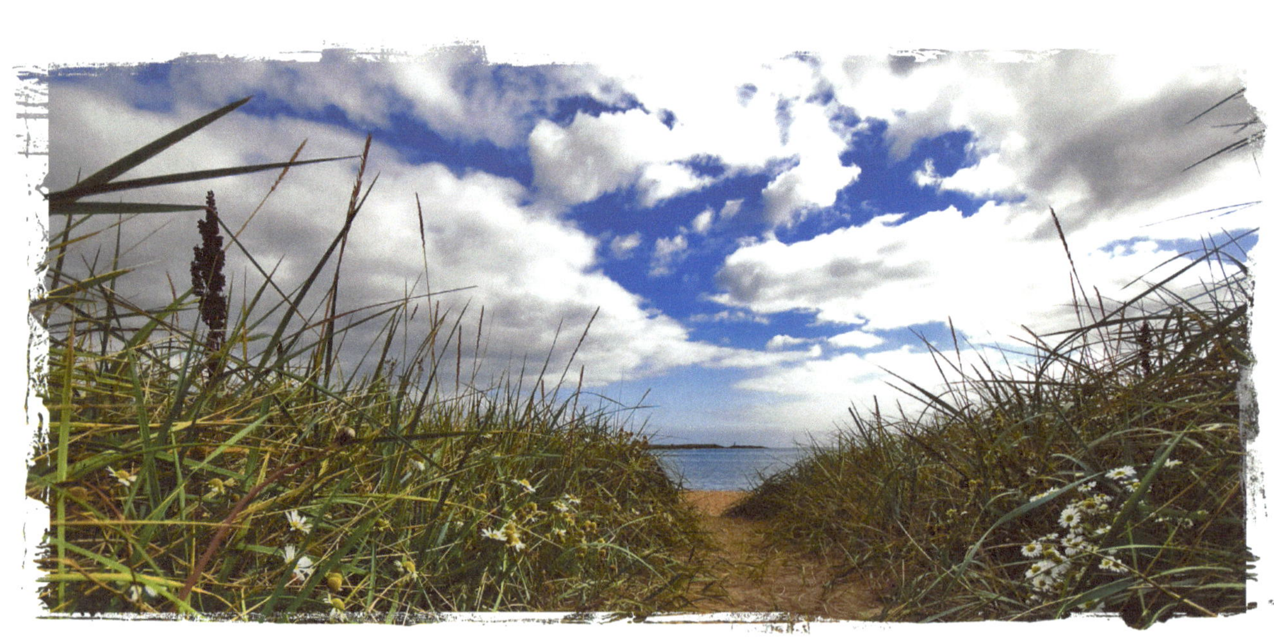

To Lose a View

Colours were stripped from my eyes, one by one! making a
view lifeless, when I thought it would live forever.

Where was the courage to invent new colours in the sky and
sea, even when it was at its darkest moment?

Where was the imagination to create darkness into light?

Where was the view who befriended two eyes that made them
now blind?

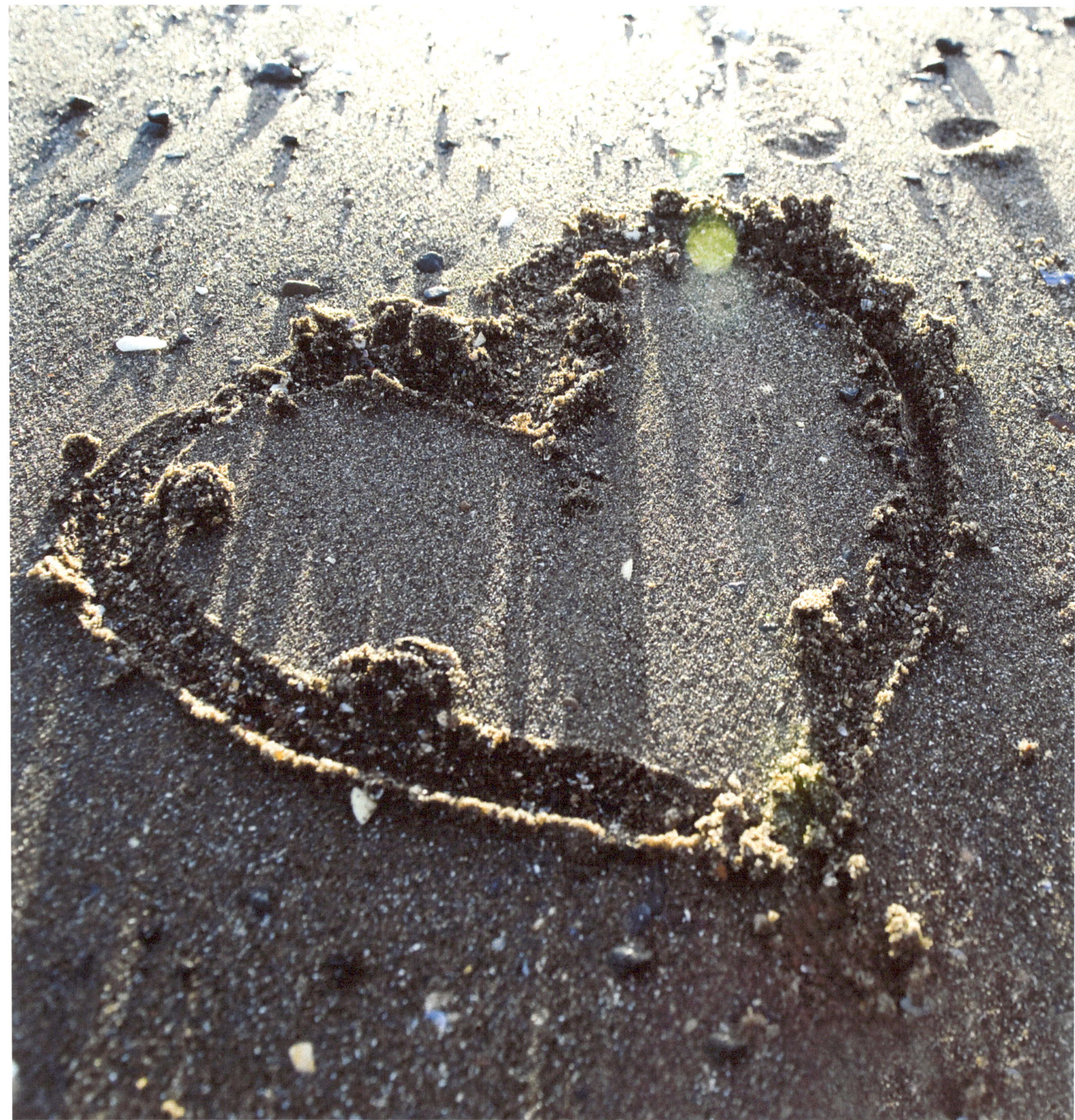

Who She is!

I want to love her more; I don't believe I can see or find a
limitation of what I want to give, or find.

When I see her, I believe she is everything I am not.

Falling in love was easy; knowing how much I love her is
impossible to understand, or control!

She doesn't know it, but she is all I have, or could ever want.
She's not a gamble, but I will give her everything anyway!

She cuddles me and forgives my blindness, which troubled
tides have left a cataract in an eye which once sparkled.

She is all I have, which is everything and more.

For Kathleen xx

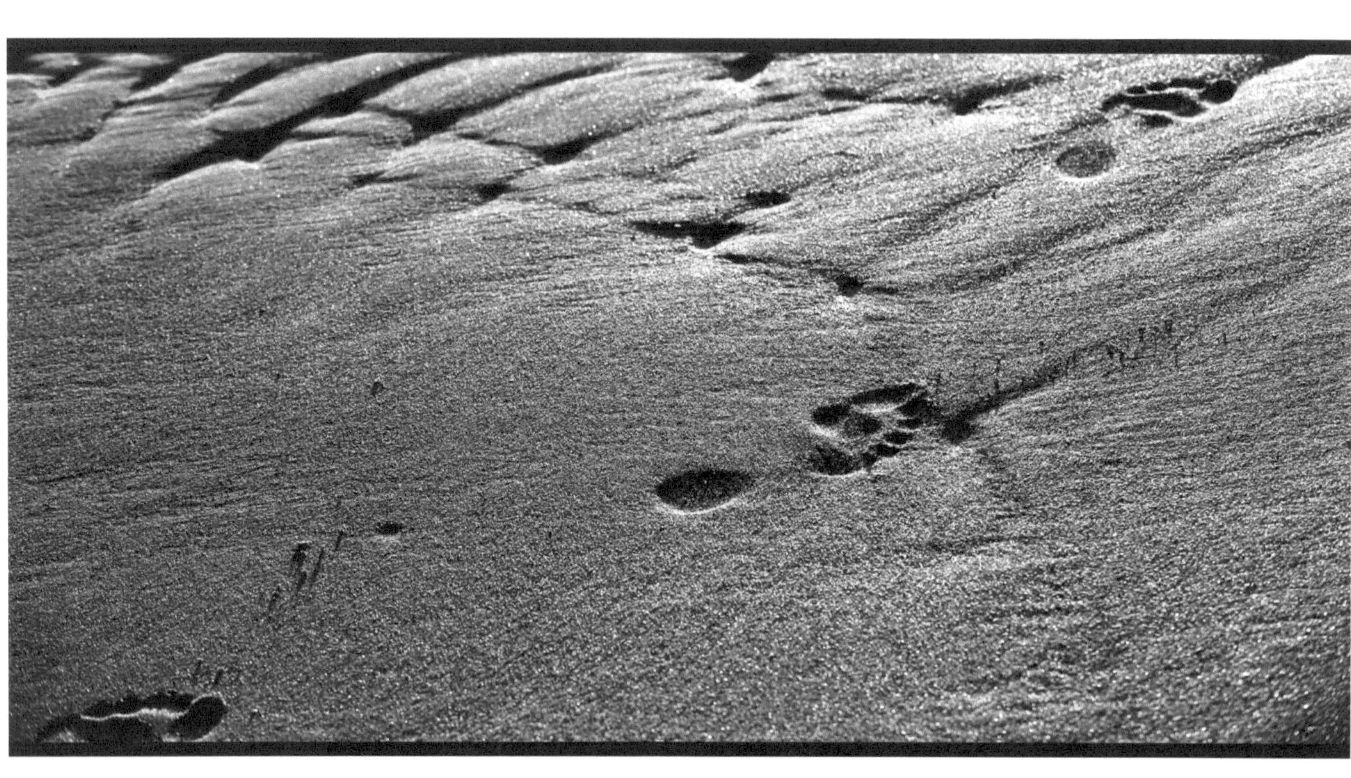

In the Wrong Place

Like a square peg, I fell into a round hole!

My grammar couldn't glue a sentence together; my voice, not for the first time, was saying the wrong things to the wrong people.

Too many mirrors were honest today, reminding me that I am me!

I was a carcass filled with question marks, awaking me every morning, demanding questions of where we are and who I was.

Friends and answers fell into shadows as black as ink, not a face or tooth could be seen.

In the wrong place with me wasn't such a bad place to be!

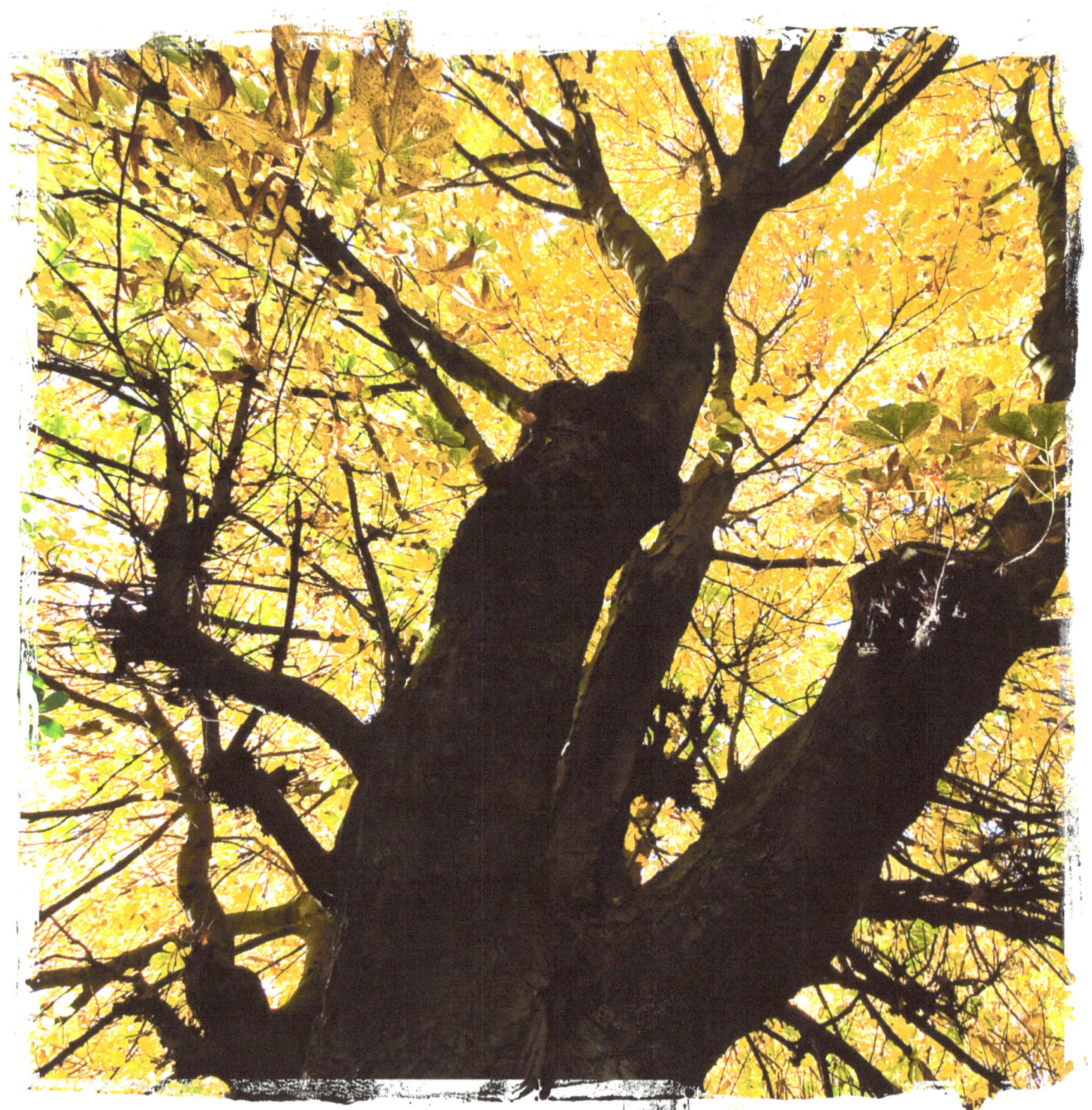

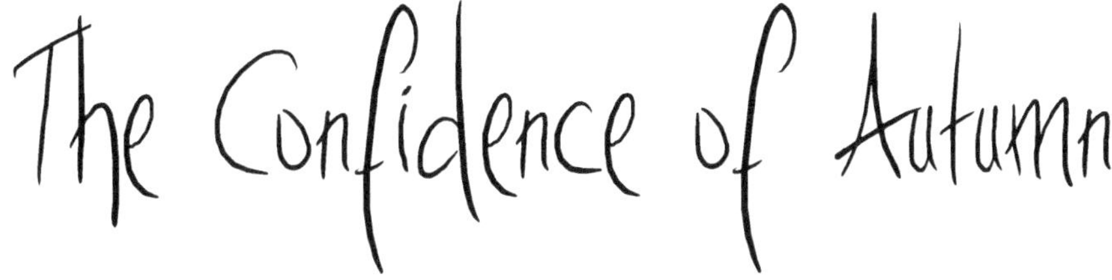

Autumn arrived, just like that!

Summer had been sacked; she had spoken like a politician for the last three months and delivered nothing. She disappointed all the colours from her pallet. Could she ever be trusted again?

The autumn's confidence grew; and as the colours of the sky recognised their new owner, a new playground crackled into life!

A cormorant danced to celebrate a new season, inches above a sea who was reminded she was now without an audience, and her own ballet should be more relaxed.

Witnessing the changes before me, I contributed a daydream, but was quickly brushed aside by a sky, which was busy changing her colours to arrange a new menu.

The confidence of the autumn, and her new colours was vast, her colours irresistible!

If only I had a paintbrush that loved me, or a dictionary that I could trust!

In the meantime, I contributed one last daydream, hoping this new season would accept me.

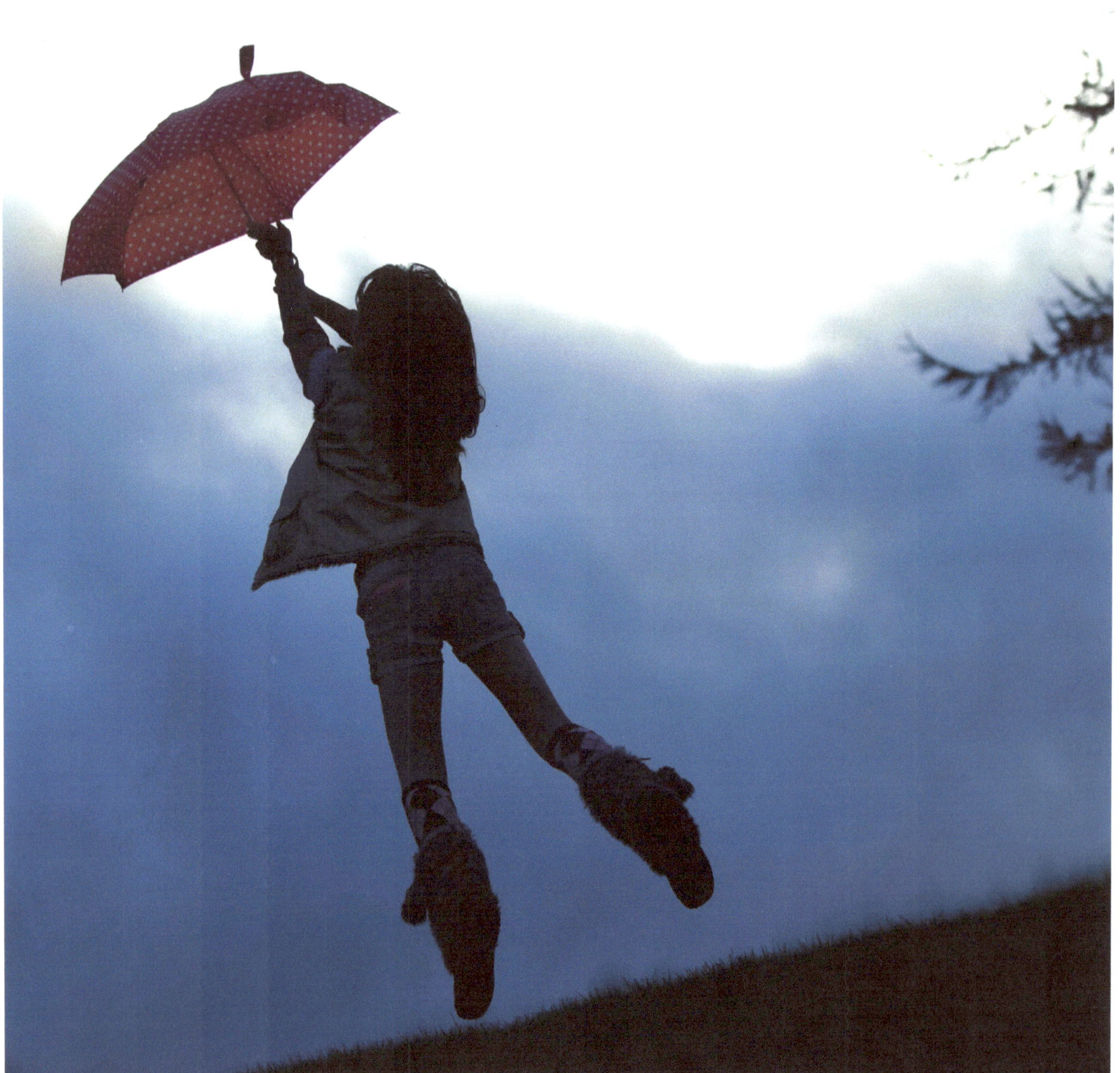

Without Darkness

With her freckles borrowed from happiness, and her olive beauty steeped in a spring-water smile, suddenly a new man was born!

This man decided no darkness should ever exist, and be banished forever while she was around.

What chance does pessimism have against a tide so deep and filled with energy, cuddles and joy, scraped from the sands of an innocent opinion?

As a bystander, I watched this young architect build my new life, brick by brick and trusting every stone she placed; she talked her way through my new building, never hesitating to explain that happiness should be fluid, and never static.

I love her more than anything!

She is the architect of cuddles and more than anything I could ever build!

For Charlie

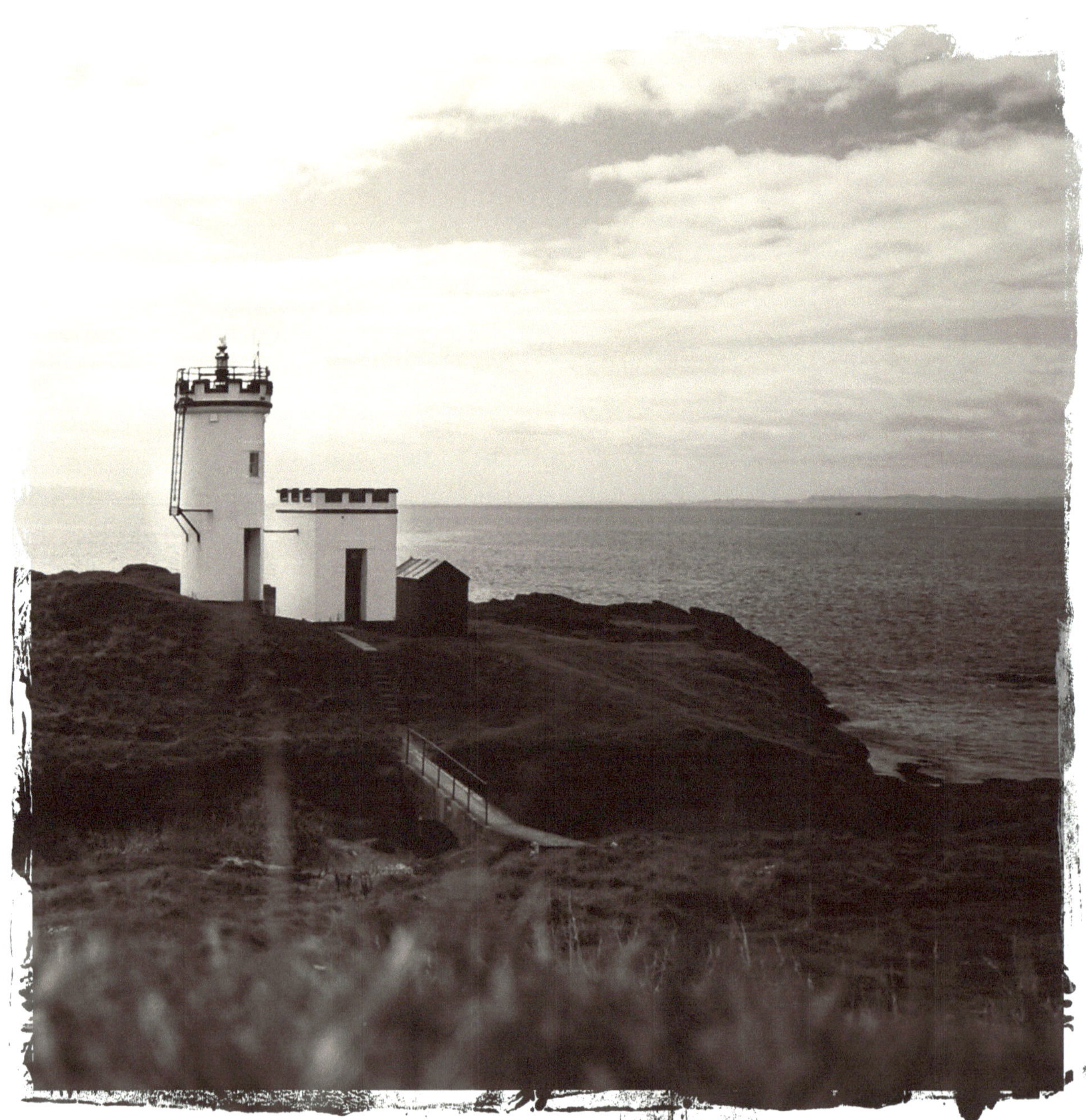

The Season Who Lied

Summer was in a bad mood.

She had tasted a season she had never ordered and, not knowing what to do, she sulked beneath a carpet of fog!

Feeling the wind's sarcasm for the first time, it became clear redundancy had never been anticipated.

Sleepless nights awaited her.

Staring onto a scene that had mistaken its timing, it brought a sadness to a season whose innocence had been lost in a sleep filled with childhood memories, blue skies and postcards never filled with love.

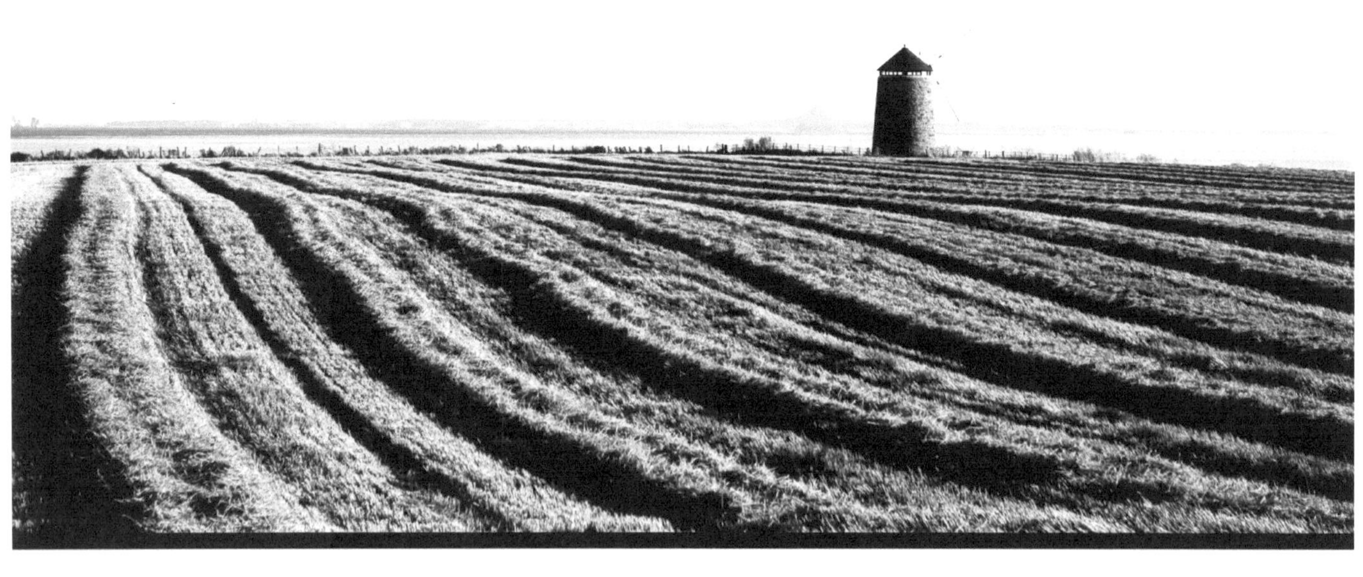

The Mood of Winter

Winter drummed her thumbs on any surface she could find; her timetable was called impatience, and today's mood stated autumn was slow and behind schedule.

Autumn was, in all honesty, trying to finish her own shift, and complete her portrait before any cold winds could challenge her thoughts or her colours.

The trees in the square had only a few fingers left; the decision of autumn had left them with a few minutes to breathe into December.

When the leaves finally made their last journey, dozens of amputated arms would point to a sky and pray for spring to be kind and come soon, to cover up their own solitude, their naked arms, and give them a purpose once again!

Dusk closed the door and locked away the light, which would now belong to no-one.

Spring was asleep and far away from anything that needed a colour or a petal.

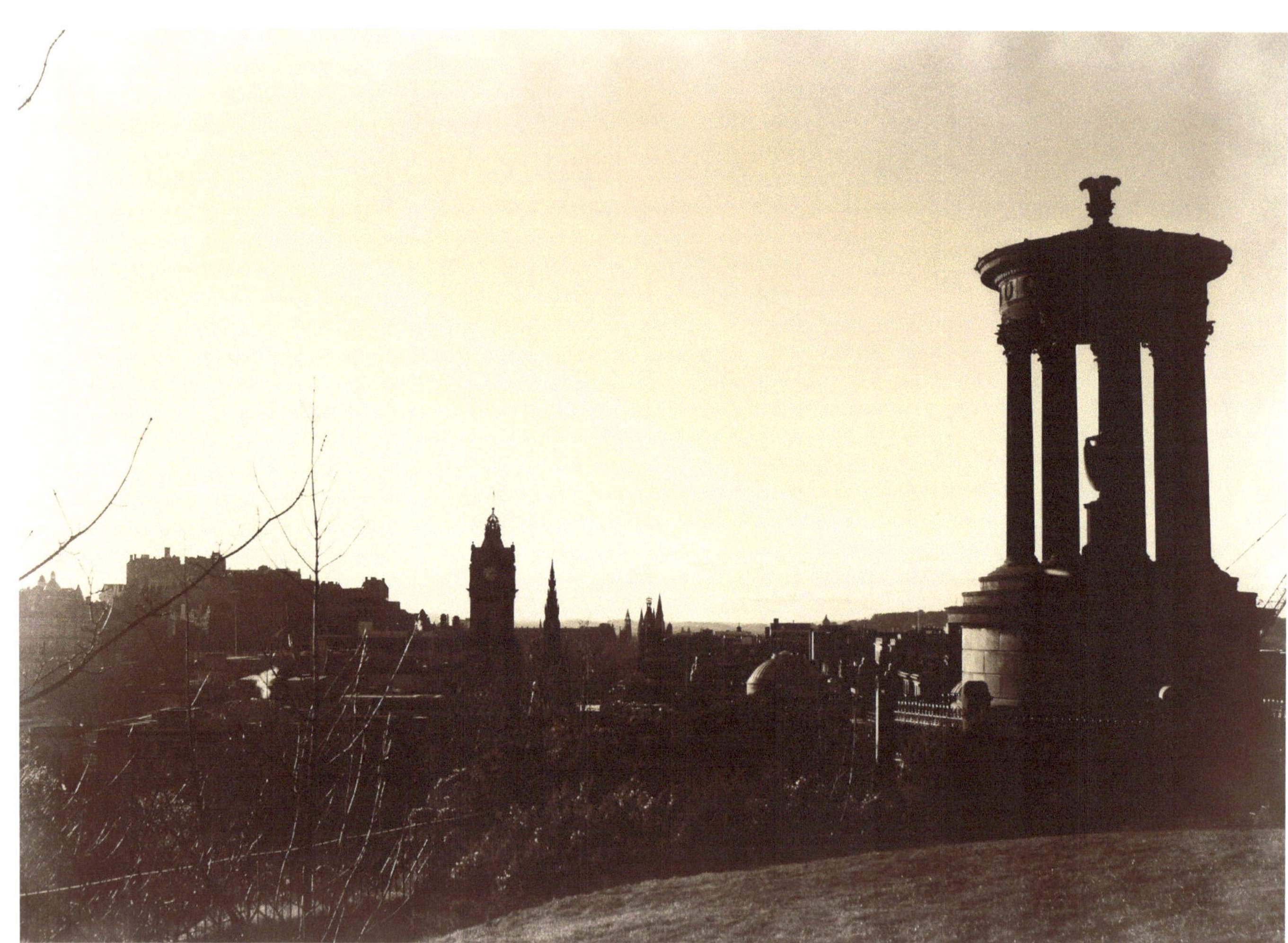

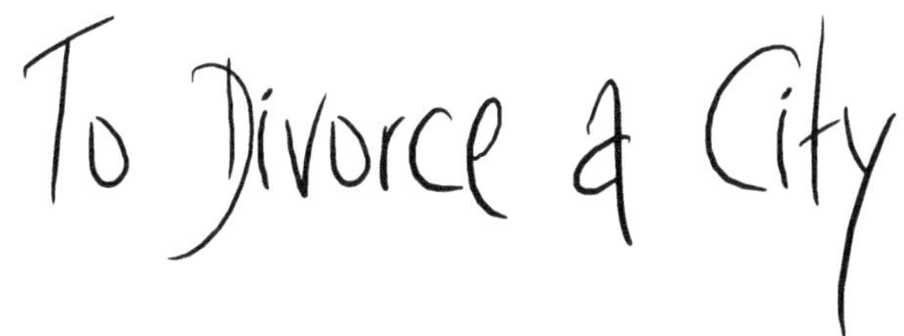

It is time to leave. I'm not sure if I am leaving you, or are you sending me away?

The result will remain the same: Are we no longer together?

Did I hurt you, or did you hurt me?

I asked only for a clear vision, perhaps a request too far, yet again!

You, in return, gave me segments of a jigsaw which you knew I could never complete!

Knowing well I had the courage to hold a hand with another, I wanted to hold your hands, with my own skin and blood, but perhaps frightened I would crush a hand that may offer me friendship!

I believe as we part company, I have given more to you than you have given to me!

You are proud and beautiful and started from nothing! I am nothing, but started from the same ambition you used to own!

So, we have this in common; why, then, do you resent me for being like you?

I leave in 12 hours. Will I miss you? putting behind me masonry, magpies and a castle! I don't know.

Let the hands of a clock judge us both together equally and measure blood for blood!

www.ingramcontent.com/pod-product-compliance
Lightning Source LLC
LaVergne TN
LVHW070221110826
845147LV00003B/617

9781909039353